ALEXANDER HAMILTON

by Meg Gaertner

Cody Koala
An Imprint of Pop!
popbooksonline.com

abdopublishing.com
Published by Pop!, a division of ABDO, PO Box 398166, Minneapolis, Minnesota 55439.

Printed in the United States of America, North Mankato, Minnesota

022018
092018
THIS BOOK CONTAINS RECYCLED MATERIALS

Cover Photo: Everett Historical/Shutterstock Images
Interior Photos: Shutterstock Images, 1, 9 (bottom right), 13, 20; Hulton Archive/Getty Images, 5, 17, 21 (top right) 21 (bottom); Library of Congress, 6, 21 (top left); North Wind Picture Archives, 9 (top), 11; Interim Archives/Getty Images, 9 (bottom left); Universal History Archive/UIG/Getty Images, 14; Carol M. Highsmith/Library of Congress, 19

Editor: Charly Haley
Series Designer: Laura Mitchell

Library of Congress Control Number: 2017963381

Publisher's Cataloging-in-Publication Data
Names: Gaertner, Meg, author.
Title: Alexander Hamilton / by Meg Gaertner.
Description: Minneapolis, Minnesota : Pop!, 2019. | Series: Founding fathers | Includes online resources and index.
Identifiers: ISBN 9781532160196 (lib.bdg.) | ISBN 9781532161315 (ebook) |
Subjects: LCSH: Hamilton, Alexander, 1757-1804--Juvenile literature. | Founding Fathers of the United States--Juvenile literature. | Statesmen- -United States--Biography--Juvenile literature. | United States--Politics and government--1783-1789--Juvenile literature.
Classification: DDC 973.4 [B]--dc23

Hello! My name is

Cody Koala

Pop open this book and you'll find QR codes like this one, loaded with information, so you can learn even more!

Scan this code* and others like it while you read, or visit the website below to make this book pop.

popbooksonline.com/alexander-hamilton

*Scanning QR codes requires a web-enabled smart device with a QR code reader app and a camera.

Table of Contents

Chapter 1
Growing Up 4

Chapter 2
War 8

Chapter 3
Shaping the New Country 12

Chapter 4
America Today 18

Making Connections 22
Glossary. 23
Index 24
Online Resources 24

Chapter 1

Growing Up

Alexander Hamilton grew up poor. His father left when he was a child. His mother died a few years later.

Watch a video here!

Alexander's childhood home

Alexander lived on an island. It was not part of the American **colonies**. He worked hard as a child. He moved to the colonies for school.

Alexander was 11 when he began working.

Chapter 2

War

Great Britain ruled the colonies. The colonies wanted to rule themselves. The **American Revolutionary War** began. Hamilton helped the colonies win the war.

Learn more here!

He aided General George Washington. The colonies became the United States. Hamilton would be a leader in the new country.

Washington
Hamilton

Chapter 3

Shaping the New Country

The **Constitution** listed the rules of the new government. But Americans did not agree on how the country should work.

Complete an activity here!

Hamilton wrote many papers to explain the Constitution. People liked what he said. They agreed to follow the Constitution.

Hamilton ran the country's **treasury**. He helped the government make money.

Hamilton had eight children.

Later Hamilton left the government to work as a lawyer. He still helped run the country.

Aaron Burr ran for president. Hamilton told people not to pick him. Burr lost the race and became angry.

Burr and Hamilton fought. Burr shot Hamilton. Hamilton died the next day.

Chapter 4

America Today

Hamilton was a **Founding Father**. He fought for the Constitution. It still guides the country today. His face can be seen on the ten-dollar bill.

THE TREASURY DEPARTMENT
Learn more here!

Hamilton helped shape the colonies into the United States. His work can still be felt today.

On January 11, Hamilton was born in Nevis, an island in the British West Indies.

1755–1757

On July 12, Hamilton died after being shot by Aaron Burr.

1804

1787–1788

Hamilton wrote papers to explain the new Constitution to the American people.

1789

Hamilton began running the treasury of the United States.

1795

Hamilton left the government to be a lawyer.

Making Connections

Text-to-Self

This book talks about Hamilton's early life. How is your life different from Hamilton's? How is it similar?

Text-to-Text

Have you read another book about a person from the past? What did you learn?

Text-to-World

Hamilton was a Founding Father. How did Hamilton's actions shape the world you live in?

Glossary

American Revolutionary War – the war fought between the colonies and Great Britain.

colony – a land ruled by another country.

Constitution – a set of rules about what the US government can do.

Founding Father – one of the people who helped create the US government.

treasury – the part of the government that controls the government's money.

Index

American Revolutionary War, 8–10

Burr, Aaron, 16–17

colonies, 7, 8–10, 20

Constitution, 12–14, 18

Great Britain, 8

treasury, 15

United States, 10, 20

Washington, George, 10

Online Resources

popbooksonline.com

Thanks for reading this Cody Koala book!

Scan this code* and others like it in this book, or visit the website below to make this book pop!

*Scanning QR codes requires a web-enabled smart device with a QR code reader app and a camera.